W9-CSM-608

Everything I Know About Life I Learned From Trash Talk TV

By

Eric Stein

CCC PUBLICATIONS

Published by:
CCC PUBLICATIONS
9725 Lurline Avenue
Chatsworth, CA 91311

Manufactured in the United States of America

Cover © 1999 CCC Publications

Cover design by Lightsource Studios

Cover & interior production Klaus Seldrede

ISBN: 1-57644-095-8

If your local U.S. bookstore is out of stock, copies of this book may be obtained by mailing check or money order for $6.95 per book (plus $2.75 to cover postage and handling) to: CCC Publications; 9725 Lurline Avenue; Chatsworth, CA 91311.

Pre-publication Edition – 8/99

Dedicated to
Jerry, Ricki,
Jenny and Sally

For

Alice & Max

Introduction

Each day the classroom of life doles out
a generous supply of wisdom from a host of
unlikely instructors that include the wind,
wildlife, waves, and even the sordid sound
bites from Trash Talk TV.

The messages these teachers impart are as
diverse as the forms they take. A tree bending
in the autumn wind demonstrates flexibility.
Bears settling in for a long winter's nap
exemplify the need for adaptability. A chair
flying through the air and slicing a three inch
gash in someone's head illustrates the impor-
tance of *insurability*.

But the chair's lesson doesn't stop there.
It leaves behind a lot more than a disfiguring
scar. As you peal back the layers of symbol-
ism and bandages, you're exposed to a
wealth of invaluable insights from which
each person can draw their own unique perspective. Someone may relate best to the idea
that: **"Sticks and stones will break your
bones, but an airborne chair will *really* mess
you up,"** while someone else may see things
more clearly with the notion that, **"Honesty
is the best policy — if you don't need all
your teeth."**

This book catalogs hundreds of these observations from the life lessons broadcast everyday from the school of hard knocks. It gives you the freedom to digest each inspiring thought at your own pace and in the privacy of your own home.

This must-have compendium will ensure you don't miss any of these invaluable, life-enriching messages. Most importantly, it will help you understand that: **"If you can't exercise restraint, you'll end up exercising in prison."**

Everything I Know About Life I Learned From Trash Talk TV

■

- Two wrongs don't make a right, but a quick left will get the point across.

- Do unto others and then do them again.

- You may never get a second chance to make it with your first cousin.

Everything I Know About Life I Learned From Trash Talk TV

- Don't stoop to someone else's level . . . when you have the opportunity to go even lower.

- If you can't say anything good about someone, don't say anything until you have an audience.

- Damned if you do, body slammed if you don't.

Everything I Know About Life
I Learned From Trash Talk TV

- Don't sweat the small stuff if you can afford implants.

- Love means never having to say you're bisexual.

- If you only scratch the surface, you're not scratching hard enough.

Everything I Know About Life
I Learned From Trash Talk TV

■

• Good news seldom follows
  the words, "Honey, I've got
  something to tell you."

• When the going gets tough,
  the tough go public.

• Nothing says "its over"
  quite like a restraining
  order.

Everything I Know About Life I Learned From Trash Talk TV

■

- A friend in need, is a friend who needs it.

- You can't keep a good man down, but a chokehold sure helps.

- Forgive and forget, but never throw away evidence you can use against them in the future.

Everything I Know About Life
I Learned From Trash Talk TV

■

- Your work force may like what they're making, but you can't force them to make it with you.

- If at first you don't succeed, try sleeping with them.

- What goes around can't always be cured.

Everything I Know About Life I Learned From Trash Talk TV

- Birds of a feather flock one another.

- You can tell a lot about a man's character by the way he carries his purse.

- You can teach your students math, but you can't help them multiply.

Everything I Know About Life
I Learned From Trash Talk TV

∎

- Even the best pair of handcuffs can't keep a couple together.

- Some things are better left in the closet.

- Nothing kills the moment like a confession.

Everything I Know About Life I Learned From Trash Talk TV

■

- Loose lips bleed.

- You can be the teacher's pet, but you can't pet the teacher.

- A picture can say a thousand words that don't sound anything like what you *actually* said.

Everything I Know About Life
I Learned From Trash Talk TV

- Make new friends and keep the old . . . on payroll.

- The only thing we have to fear is getting caught.

- Time will tell ALL.

Everything I Know About Life
I Learned From Trash Talk TV

- What a good alibi giveth, positive DNA results taketh away.

- Never bite off more than you can chew, unless you can swallow it whole.

- Don't get mad, get airtime.

Everything I Know About Life I Learned From Trash Talk TV

- Where there's a will, there's someone waiting to contest it.

- It's hard to know who wears the pants in a cross-dresser's family.

- Misery loves company, polygamy loves *lots* of it.

Everything I Know About Life I Learned From Trash Talk TV

- It only takes a little dirt to really clean up.

- A double-digit IQ is the single most important reason to take the Fifth.

- Never waste an opportunity to tell someone you'd love to kill them.

Everything I Know About Life
I Learned From Trash Talk TV

• One man's trash is another man's girlfriend.

• Get everything out on the table . . . except for the breakables.

• Familiarity breeds.

Everything I Know About Life
I Learned From Trash Talk TV

- If you can't get someone to embrace your position, try a headlock.

- The best things in life are free-for-alls.

- Thou shall not covet thy neighbor's wife, but thy neighbor's husband is fair game.

Everything I Know About Life
I Learned From Trash Talk TV

■

- If you are caught with your pants down, you could lose your shirt.

- No one knows what goes on behind closed doors, but after today they'll have a much better idea.

- A little surgery goes a long way.

Everything I Know About Life I Learned From Trash Talk TV

■

- A broken nose is nothing to sneeze at.

- Don't put off till tomorrow, what you can take off today.

- Thou shall not bear falsies.

Everything I Know About Life
I Learned From Trash Talk TV

■

- Nothing ventured,
  nothing sprained.

- Time heals all . . . but
  traction and intensive care
  really help.

- Your two cents may get
  you quartered.

Everything I Know About Life I Learned From Trash Talk TV

- The truth is hard to swallow, but it goes down much easier than a knuckle sandwich.

- When in Rome, do the Romans.

- Humble pie can leave a bad taste in your mouth.

Everything I Know About Life
I Learned From Trash Talk TV

■

- A loaded question will blow up in your face.

- Come home with rug burns and you'll get called on the carpet.

- A penny for your thoughts may be more than they're worth.

Everything I Know About Life I Learned From Trash Talk TV

- If push comes to shove, do both.

- What may strike you funny, may strike you back.

- Just because someone gives you the slip, doesn't mean you have to put it on.

Everything I Know About Life I Learned From Trash Talk TV

- Free speech can be *very* costly.

- A public forum can damage your privates.

- Scratching a seven year itch can leave you scarred for life.

Everything I Know About Life
I Learned From Trash Talk TV

- Quit while you're ahead, and you won't have to take it in the behind.

- The sweetest revenge is giving someone their just desserts.

- Some people get all the breaks . . . and unfortunately they seldom have major medical.

Everything I Know About Life
I Learned From Trash Talk TV

■

- Massaging the truth rubs people the wrong way.

- Hindsight is twenty-twenty . . . but oversight can get you twenty to life.

- Give someone the short end of the stick, and they will stick it to you.

Everything I Know About Life I Learned From Trash Talk TV

■

- Do your best, but *don't* do your best man.

- If pulling some strings doesn't work, try pulling some hair.

- If you can still hear the chainsaw, you're not out of the woods.

Everything I Know About Life I Learned From Trash Talk TV

■

- The squeaky wheel gets the tire iron.

- Nothing delivers, like *black*mail.

- Bruised egos heal much faster than broken bones.

Everything I Know About Life
I Learned From Trash Talk TV

▪

- The truth will set you free
  . . . until you're sentenced.

- Only a postal worker can
  deliver mail, but anyone
  can go *postal*.

- The skeletons in your closet
  often come out before you do.

Everything I Know About Life
I Learned From Trash Talk TV

■

- Ask a penetrating question and you'll get a pregnant pause.

- The path of least resistance is no free ride, but the *beaten* path always takes a toll.

- It's the gray areas that can leave you black and blue.

Everything I Know About Life I Learned From Trash Talk TV

■

- Laughter is the best medicine . . . unless you score some really good painkillers.

- The best offense is a good defense *attorney*.

- If it ain't broke, it soon will be.

Everything I Know About Life I Learned From Trash Talk TV

■

- Practice what you preach, but don't practice it with the preacher.

- If they throw the book at you, you'll have plenty of time to read it.

- If you can't strike a happy medium, strike whoever's closest.

30

Everything I Know About Life I Learned From Trash Talk TV

■

- When you're greeted with open arms, don't open fire.

- The truth hurts . . . but not as much as a good slap in the face.

- You can dress him up, but you can't take him out in women's underwear.

Everything I Know About Life I Learned From Trash Talk TV

■

- If someone has an ax to grind, it could cost you an arm and a leg.

- If you have a window of opportunity . . . close the curtains first.

- You can kick someone out of the club, but you can't dismember them.

Everything I Know About Life
I Learned From Trash Talk TV

■

- An ounce of prevention
  can keep you from getting
  pounded.

- You scratch my back and I'll
  scratch your eyes out.

- Confession is good for
  the soul, but it can be
  hazardous to the flesh.

Everything I Know About Life I Learned From Trash Talk TV

■

- Good things are rarely on tap, when they come from the bottom of the barrel.

- It's not over till you're six feet under.

- Don't give someone a piece of your mind, when you don't have enough to spare.

Everything I Know About Life
I Learned From Trash Talk TV

■

- Good things come to those who wait, but they come a lot faster if you throw your weight around.

- Love thy neighbor . . . but at your own risk.

- Experience is the best teacher, but a really good teacher gives *you* the best experience.

Everything I Know About Life I Learned From Trash Talk TV

∎

- Nailing your handyman's spouse will get you hammered.

- Good friends are hard to find . . . *especially* when they owe you money.

- Love will find a way, but it's usually while you're *away* on business.

Everything I Know About Life I Learned From Trash Talk TV

■

- Offer the olive branch *before* you're up a tree.

- An attitude adjusted today, is a nose that won't have to be set tomorrow.

- It's hard to be a picture of good health . . . when you mess with someone in a bad frame of mind.

Everything I Know About Life
I Learned From Trash Talk TV

■

- Don't wear your heart on your sleeve or lipstick on your collar.

- Rattle someone's cage and you could end up behind bars.

- Give someone an inch . . . and they'll never give you *any*, again.

Everything I Know About Life
I Learned From Trash Talk TV

- There is a time and place for every *fling*.

- What slips your mind may trip you up.

- Rules are made to be broken, but not necessarily over someone's head.

Everything I Know About Life
I Learned From Trash Talk TV

■

- It's only off the record till it's on the air.

- If someone's in a blind rage, stay out of sight.

- Be thankful for what you've got and pray you don't get what you deserve.

Everything I Know About Life
I Learned From Trash Talk TV

- No one creases the sheets like a center*fold*.

- Fits happen.

- You're innocent until beaten silly.

Everything I Know About Life
I Learned From Trash Talk TV

■

- Never let your left hand
  know *who* your right hand
  is doing.

- Two in the bush can get
  out of hand.

- The last straw really sucks.

Everything I Know About Life I Learned From Trash Talk TV

■

- One step *sister* at a time.

- Beauty is in the eyes of your cellmate.

- Wonders never cease . . . until you get the cease and desist order.

Everything I Know About Life
I Learned From Trash Talk TV

■

- Someone who shows you the ropes should be well hung.

- Losing your head won't get you any tail.

- It's not whether you win or lose, its how you place the blame.

Everything I Know About Life
I Learned From Trash Talk TV

- You can blow off steam, but blowing anything else will bring you to your knees.

- If you *think* you're beaten, you weren't beaten *long* enough.

- A sound body, sounds good.

Everything I Know About Life
I Learned From Trash Talk TV

■

- If you have to ask the price . . . you can't afford her.

- Ears are something you can really sink your teeth into.

- People who need people are *needy* people.

Everything I Know About Life
I Learned From Trash Talk TV

- Holding a grudge is not
  as effective as holding
  a hostage.

- A love triangle can be a
  vicious circle.

- When gravity takes hold . . .
  men let go.

Everything I Know About Life I Learned From Trash Talk TV

- Don't get all torn apart just because someone rips you a new one.

- People beaten to the punch are *sore* losers.

- Opposites attack.

Everything I Know About Life
I Learned From Trash Talk TV

■

- Give it to jail bait today . . . get it from a cellmate tomorrow.

- Politics makes strange bedfellows, but not as strange as the fellows they're in bed with.

- The grass is always greener . . . when someone's rubbing your face in it.

Everything I Know About Life I Learned From Trash Talk TV

■

- Don't get slap happy with the *SWAT* team.

- If you mess with forbidden you'll end up a bedridden vegetable.

- When opportunity comes knocking, don't let it knock you up.

Everything I Know About Life
I Learned From Trash Talk TV

- Your babysitter may have a way with kids, but you can't have your way with the babysitter.

- You'll *get* better under a nurse's care, but you'll *feel* better under the nurse.

- Don't shoot the breeze if you're loaded.

Everything I Know About Life I Learned From Trash Talk TV

- Never underestimate an overactive imagination.

- Don't pour salt in an open wound . . . unless you're out of pepper spray.

- Don't start any*one* you can't finish.

Everything I Know About Life
I Learned From Trash Talk TV

- Absence makes the heart grow fonder, for *whoever's* in your presence.

- Don't grab at straws . . . when you can just as easily go for the throat.

- What you see is what you get . . . unless someone neglected to mention they had a sex change.

Everything I Know About Life
I Learned From Trash Talk TV

■

- May the best man *sin*.

- Come all ye faithful, but don't come too quickly.

- Accentuate the positive *only* when the test results come back negative.

Everything I Know About Life
I Learned From Trash Talk TV

■

- There's no business like someone else's business.

- The way to a man's heart is through his ribcage.

- Stand up and be mounted.

Everything I Know About Life
I Learned From Trash Talk TV

■

- Do your own thing, but don't do it on video.

- If you churn someone else's butter, you'll get creamed.

- Biting comments leave lasting impressions.

Everything I Know About Life I Learned From Trash Talk TV

■

- If you can make out here . . . you can make out anywhere.

- If you cast the first stone, don't miss.

- Even the best-*laid* plans can get you *screwed*.

Everything I Know About Life
I Learned From Trash Talk TV

■

- There's nothing new under the son . . . except for his mother-in-law.

- Laughing in someone's face will have you in stitches.

- It's not over till the fat lady sits on you.

Everything I Know About Life
I Learned From Trash Talk TV

■

- Don't go back for seconds when you get the *third* degree.

- All good things must come to a head.

- If you can't add anything constructive . . . ad nauseam.

Everything I Know About Life I Learned From Trash Talk TV

■

- The easiest way to get to "yes," is to get to someone who's easy.

- Expose yourself to ridicule and you'll pay a price, but expose it *all* — and they'll pay you.

- Stand by your mannequin.

Everything I Know About Life I Learned From Trash Talk TV

■

- If you can't take the heat, don't do it in the sauna.

- You can sever a relationship, but you can't cut *it* off.

- Speak softly and carry a tape recorder.

Everything I Know About Life
I Learned From Trash Talk TV

■

- You can't argue with success
  . . . or heavily armed
  security guards either.

- Father knows best, but mom
  knows the *mailman*.

- Know when to cut your
  losses, but don't use a
  chainsaw.

Everything I Know About Life I Learned From Trash Talk TV

■

- God moves in mysterious ways . . . but an exotic dancer's moves are *truly* divine.

- It takes less time to go up the corporate ladder, if you spend more time going *down* on the CEO.

- You can't please all the people all the time . . . unless you're extremely well endowed.

63

Everything I Know About Life I Learned From Trash Talk TV

■

- Reach out and touch someone . . . but only *after* you've seen their test results.

- There's safety in numchucks.

- You get what you pay for . . . but you *really* pay for what you *didn't* count on getting.

Everything I Know About Life I Learned From Trash Talk TV

- Giving someone the bird will *always* ruffle their feathers.

- Time flies . . . as do chairs, china and other household items.

- You can't judge a book by its cover girl.

Everything I Know About Life I Learned From Trash Talk TV

- He who does nice things for you now . . . expects you to do the *nasty* with *him* later.

- Love conquers all, but hate gives it a good run for the money.

- Knowledge is power: carnal knowledge is a good way to lose it.

Everything I Know About Life
I Learned From Trash Talk TV

■

- Air your dirty laundry and someone may take you to the cleaners.

- It's better to have egg on your face . . . than to have your face scrambled.

- It only takes a few words to make a life sentence.

Everything I Know About Life
I Learned From Trash Talk TV

- With friends like these, who needs edible underwear.

- Impatience breeds inpatients.

- If you've got it, flog it.

Everything I Know About Life
I Learned From Trash Talk TV

■

- You know you've worn out
  your welcome . . . when
  your face becomes the
  welcome mat.

- The bigger they are, the
  harder they maul.

- If someone calls your bluff
  . . . call 911.

Everything I Know About Life
I Learned From Trash Talk TV

■

- The meek shall inhabit
  the ER.

- Step out of line . . . and
  you could end up in the
  line of fire.

- Before you mouth off, make
  sure there is a doctor on call.

Everything I Know About Life I Learned From Trash Talk TV

■

- All men are cremated equal.

- You don't necessarily have to get out of your clothes . . . to get something off your chest.

- The dirt you dig up may used to bury you.

Everything I Know About Life
I Learned From Trash Talk TV

■

- Doing it with your Major is nothing minor, but making it with a *Medium* is out of this world.

- You can't get blood from a stone . . . but a stone *always* gets the blood flowing.

- If your timing is really bad, someone may clean your clock.

Everything I Know About Life
I Learned From Trash Talk TV

■

- You can lay it on the line . . . but a really good line can get you laid.

- Hold your horses or some- one may fix your wagon.

- If you go against the grain, you could end up in a splinter group.

Everything I Know About Life I Learned From Trash Talk TV

■

- A hired gun gives you more bang for your buck.

- Marriages are made in heaven . . . affairs are made in hotels.

- You can't always find your way, but find someone who's willing — and you can go *all* the way.

Everything I Know About Life
I Learned From Trash Talk TV

■

- It's not what you know, it's who knows you know it and what they'll pay you to keep quiet.

- Make love not warrants.

- You can tell a man by the concubine he keeps.

Everything I Know About Life
I Learned From Trash Talk TV

- Let bygones be bygones . . . until the witnesses have gone by.

- Just because you take some-one under your wing . . . doesn't mean you can take them under the covers.

- Those who can't live in the lap of luxury, can live pretty well if they lap dance.

Everything I Know About Life I Learned From Trash Talk TV

- People who don't want to come out of the closet, need to keep their story *straight*.

- You don't have to be a doctor to get a taste of your own medicine . . . but you may need one when you do.

- The time for good behavior is *before* you're behind bars.

Everything I Know About Life
I Learned From Trash Talk TV

■

- Another day, another *broken* collar.

- Money can't buy love, but it can buy some *really* naughty toys.

- Seeing is believing . . . that is, until you see your blind date.

Everything I Know About Life
I Learned From Trash Talk TV

■

- You can cut all ties with your family, but remember to *untie* them first.

- It's the unfinished business that will finish you off.

- Some people can only see your perspective . . . *after* they see your mace.

Everything I Know About Life
I Learned From Trash Talk TV

■

- Any*one* worth doing is worth doing again.

- Mind your own business . . . record everyone else's.

- Thou shall not kilt.

Everything I Know About Life
I Learned From Trash Talk TV

- Black is beautiful, but black and blue is another story.

- Count your blessings, but don't count them 'till you're safely in your car.

- Don't tie the knot with anyone . . . who has you on the ropes.

Everything I Know About Life
I Learned From Trash Talk TV

■

- You don't have to touch anyone else, to get in touch with your feminine side.

- You can draw your own conclusions, but you don't have to tattoo them on your forehead.

- Laughter is contagious, but it's nothing that a swift kick can't cure.

Everything I Know About Life
I Learned From Trash Talk TV

■

- Figures never lie . . . but good figures *always* get laid.

- You can handle a situation diplomatically, but handle the diplomat — and you've got a *difficult* situation.

- You can make it with someone from your past, but don't make it with someone who has passed on.

Everything I Know About Life
I Learned From Trash Talk TV

■

- If you see someone on the side, you may suffer some side effects.

- There's no harm in asking, except when you're asking for trouble.

- It's hard to till the field without a *hoe*, but it's easy to *play* the field if you are *one*.

Everything I Know About Life
I Learned From Trash Talk TV

- Breaking up is hard to do, and it's even *harder* when you're having a breakdown.

- It's difficult to date strippers due to the on-again, off-again nature of their work.

- You can throw caution to the wind, but don't throw *him* through the window.

Everything I Know About Life
I Learned From Trash Talk TV

▨

- It's hard to let conscience be your guide, when you don't have one to begin with.

- You can dress for success, but *undress* and you'll really be successful.

- Parishioners seek forgiveness for the sins they've done, clergy seek parishioners for sins yet to come.

86

Everything I Know About Life
I Learned From Trash Talk TV

- The show must go on, but *you* don't have to go on the show.

- Give credit where credit is due, but use cash if you don't want to get caught.

- You are what you eat . . . but you're remembered by what you swallow.

About the Author

■

Eric Stein, a 1995-96 regional finalist for a White House Fellowship, has written for a European children's television series, penned numerous award-winning radio, TV and print ads and was a supervising producer on a special for the Fox Children's Network. A former NBC page who handed Johnny Carson prize envelopes on the Tonight Show, Stein now heads his own entertainment licensing company which does merchandising for various television, film and record companies and develops entertainment programming.

Stein, who graduated Phi Kappa Phi from the University of Arizona, acknowledges some benefits of having a degree, but feels the value of his may have been diminished by the fact that Geraldo graduated from the U. of A. as well. Although he confesses it took him seven years to graduate, Stein credits Regis Philbin with guilting him back to school in a conversation he had with him during his three year academic hiatus at NBC.

Stein grew up in Madison, WI and believes his interest in television was probably spurred by his mom's decision to make their household TV-less. While he feels that some may find that a bit strange, he doesn't think it's as odd as growing up lactose intolerant in the Dairy State.

Stein, 39, lives in Marina del Rey, California.

TITLES BY CCC PUBLICATIONS

Blank Books ($3.99)
GUIDE TO SEX AFTER BABY
GUIDE TO SEX AFTER 30
GUIDE TO SEX AFTER 40
GUIDE TO SEX AFTER 50
GUIDE TO SEX AFTER MARRIAGE

Retail $4.95 – $4.99
"?" book
LAST DIET BOOK YOU'LL EVER NEED
CAN SEX IMPROVE YOUR GOLF?
THE COMPLETE BOOGER BOOK
FLYING FUNNIES
MARITAL BLISS & OXYMORONS
THE ADULT DOT-TO-DOT BOOK
THE DEFINITIVE FART BOOK
THE COMPLETE WIMP'S GUIDE TO SEX
THE CAT OWNER'S SHAPE UP MANUAL
THE OFFICE FROM HELL
FITNESS FANATICS
YOUNGER MEN ARE BETTER THAN RETIN-A
BUT OSSIFER, IT'S NOT MY FAULT
YOU KNOW YOU'RE AN OLD FART WHEN...
1001 WAYS TO PROCRASTINATE
HORMONES FROM HELL II
SHARING THE ROAD WITH IDIOTS
THE GREATEST ANSWERING MACHINE MESSAGES
WHAT DO WE DO NOW??
HOW TO TALK YOU WAY OUT OF A TRAFFIC TICKET
THE BOTTOM HALF
LIFE'S MOST EMBARRASSING MOMENTS
HOW TO ENTERTAIN PEOPLE YOU HATE
YOUR GUIDE TO CORPORATE SURVIVAL
NO HANG-UPS (Volumes I, II & III – $3.95 ea.)
TOTALLY OUTRAGEOUS BUMPER-SNICKERS ($2.95)

Retail $5.95
30 – DEAL WITH IT!
40 – DEAL WITH IT!
50 – DEAL WITH IT!
60 – DEAL WITH IT!
OVER THE HILL – DEAL WITH IT!
SLICK EXCUSES FOR STUPID SCREW-UPS
SINGLE WOMEN VS. MARRIED WOMEN
TAKE A WOMAN'S WORD FOR IT
SEXY CROSSWORD PUZZLES
SO, YOU'RE GETTING MARRIED
YOU KNOW HE'S A WOMANIZING SLIMEBALL WHEN...
GETTING OLD SUCKS
WHY GOD MAKES BALD GUYS
OH BABY!
PMS CRAZED: TOUCH ME AND I'LL KILL YOU!
WHY MEN ARE CLUELESS
THE BOOK OF WHITE TRASH
THE ART OF MOONING
GOLFAHOLICS
CRINKLED 'N' WRINKLED
SMART COMEBACKS FOR STUPID QUESTIONS
YIKES! IT'S ANOTHER BIRTHDAY

SEX IS A GAME
SEX AND YOUR STARS
SIGNS YOUR SEX LIFE IS DEAD
MALE BASHING: WOMEN'S FAVORITE PASTIME
THINGS YOU CAN DO WITH A USELESS MAN
MORE THINGS YOU CAN DO WITH A USELESS MAN
RETIREMENT: THE GET EVEN YEARS
LITTLE INSTRUCTION BOOK OF THE RICH & FAMOUS
WELCOME TO YOUR MIDLIFE CRISIS
GETTING EVEN WITH THE ANSWERING MACHINE
ARE YOU A SPORTS NUT?
MEN ARE PIGS / WOMEN ARE BITCHES
THE BETTER HALF
ARE WE DYSFUNCTIONAL YET?
TECHNOLOGY BYTES!
50 WAYS TO HUSTLE YOUR FRIENDS
HORMONES FROM HELL
HUSBANDS FROM HELL
KILLER BRAS & Other Hazards Of The 50's
IT'S BETTER TO BE OVER THE HILL THAN UNDER IT
HOW TO REALLY PARTY!!!
WORK SUCKS!
THE PEOPLE WATCHER'S FIELD GUIDE
THE ABSOLUTE LAST CHANCE DIET BOOK
THE UGLY TRUTH ABOUT MEN
NEVER A DULL CARD
THE LITTLE BOOK OF ROMANTIC LIES

Retail $6.95
EVERYTHING I KNOW I LEARNED FROM TRASH TALK TV
IN A PERFECT WORLD
I WISH I DIDN'T...
THE TOILET ZONE
SIGNS/TOO MUCH TIME W/CAT
LOVE & MARRIAGE & DIVORCE
CYBERGEEK IS CHIC
THE DIFFERENCE BETWEEN MEN AND WOMEN
GO TO HEALTH!
NOT TONIGHT, DEAR, I HAVE A COMPUTER!
THINGS YOU WILL NEVER HEAR THEM SAY
THE SENIOR CITIZENS'S SURVIVAL GUIDE
IT'S A MAD MAD MAD SPORTS WORLD
THE LITTLE BOOK OF CORPORATE LIES
RED HOT MONOGAMY
LOVE DAT CAT
HOW TO SURVIVE A JEWISH MOTHER

Retail $7.95
WHY MEN DON'T HAVE A CLUE
LADIES, START YOUR ENGINES!
ULI STEIN'S "ANIMAL LIFE"
ULI STEIN'S "I'VE GOT IT BUT IT'S JAMMED"
ULI STEIN'S "THAT SHOULD NEVER HAVE HAPPENED"

NO HANG-UPS – CASSETTES Retail $5.98

Vol. I:	GENERAL MESSAGES (M or F)
Vol. II:	BUSINESS MESSAGES (M or F)
Vol. III:	'R' RATED MESSAGES (M or F)
Vol. V:	CELEBRI-TEASE